Contents

Introduction	03
Getting Ready	04
• *Work Surfaces*	04
• *Tools & Materials*	05
• *Overview of Cloth & Media*	05
Making your Mark	06
• *Scraping*	06
• *Writing, Doodling, Sketching & Dragging*	09
• *Mono Printing: Four Approaches*	15
• *Painting & Dry Brushing*	21
• *Rolling*	26
• *Spraying & Streaking*	27
• *Using Found Objects*	29
• *Combining Approaches*	32
• *Finding the Time*	33
What Next?	35
• *Formats*	35
• *Reviewing & Auditioning*	37
Media & Recipes	39
• *Preparing the Cloth*	39
• *The Role of the Dye*	40
• *The Role of Soda Ash*	40
• *Making Chemical Water*	41
• *Making Print Paste*	41
• *Making Dye Paints*	42
• *Colour Mixing*	43
• *Changing Value*	43
• *Changing Consistency*	44
• *Changing Vaule & Consistency*	44
• *Curing/Batching & Rinsing*	45
• *Discharge Paste*	47
• *Fabric Paints*	48
• *Resists*	49
Resources/Suppliers	50
Further Reading	51
About Committed to Cloth	53

Introduction

Many books are available on surface design – we've already written four and co-authored two more with Jane Dunnewold. So why this book?

We're well aware that when we're teaching, many students – particularly those new to surface design – are eagerly anticipating the silkscreen and thermofax screen. We have a sense that once exposed to these tools, they feel the cloth of their dreams will magically materialise.

There's some truth in this. The silkscreen and thermofax do make it easier to bring personal imagery alive on cloth, and paper and fine line design is particularly achievable with the thermofax. However, we've noticed that students can become dependent on these tools and forget the magic of working with more mundane items such as scrapers, rollers, squeeze bottles, bits of plastic and so forth. It's as if the silkscreen and thermofax are the handsome swans – sexier, faster and more immediate - and the other tools are the Ugly Ducklings - ordinary, slower and more labour intensive.

This is a shame. We're NOT saying forgo the screen and the thermofax. Far from it. But we ARE saying "don't forget the simpler tools". With practise and imagination they're capable of producing imagery and marks that somehow come from a more direct sense of the hand. Their simplicity carries power in that no mark made can ever be exactly repeated. This inability to exactly replicate a mark can generate work that has a real sense of energy… and it will never look machine-made. Let's face it, the motivation to explore surface design usually comes from a desire to move away from using commercially produced fabric.

Using the approaches described in this book will enable you to create beautiful personal cloth - perfect backgrounds for additional imagery, stitch or embroidery - or ready to use as garment or interiors yardage. And if you're into collage or quilt-making the cloth will make a great contribution to a palette for cutting and re-structuring.

So, we'd like to encourage you to pick up some tools that may have been lingering in drawers, and enter the hardware shop or pet shop with an eye to what might be achieved with a simple paintbrush, a plastic grass doormat, a scraper, or a squeeze bottle.

We recommend you start by watching the DVD. You'll see how we use the same tool in different ways to achieve different results. You'll also get a feel for our technique before developing your own approaches. Then read – or at least browse – the book from cover to cover. The photographs of samples, works-in-progress and finished pieces will hopefully inspire you as to the possibilities. Then, select a tool you respond to and get going – perhaps watch the appropriate section of the DVD again before you start.

As you progress, remind yourself that using any tool takes practise. At first you may experience frustration; the bottle may drip or squirt in an irritating manner, the paint may blob and smear in ways you didn't expect. Remember; it's not the tool alone that makes the mark. YOU make the mark with your intention and your hand. The tool is your instrument and it'll take a while to master it. Give each tool AT LEAST 15 minutes of use before you throw it out in frustration. We've observed that after about 15 minutes, the eye, hand, brain and tool become connected and you find your flow.

Observe what's happening as you work as there are many variables:

- how you hold the tool
- how you load it with media
- the consistency of media needed
- the way you use it (stamp, stipple, drag, pounce, dab, paint, scrape)
- the pressure you apply
- the speed at which you work
- where you work from; wrist, arm, shoulder

Ultimately you're seeking to build a relationship with the tool, the media and the cloth, and mastery of them. It's worth noting that the potential of each approach is only limited by your curiosity and imagination. All of this takes time and practise… so get to it.

Layers of mark-making by Jane Willoughby-Scott

Getting Ready

The approaches in this book enable you to explore a variety of different tools and media. Some are messier than others but if you don't have a studio, don't worry. We both started our explorations in the kitchen – it just takes a little planning and you're ready for the off. In good weather, we transferred our activities to a worktable in the garden and if you do this, try to work in a shady spot so the media doesn't dry out too quickly.

If you're inside, it can help to lay down a decorator's cloth or a couple of old sheets you can wash and re-use. You won't worry so much about drips and spills and get more adventurous in your approach. You'll also need somewhere to wash tools and for most of the approaches in this book, a kitchen sink is more than adequate. A reasonable alternative is a large plastic box parked outside near a drain, filled with water from a hose or bucket. Place the box on a small picnic table so you don't have to bend.

Work Surfaces
Ideally, you want the top of your work table to be at the height of your pubic bone; about kitchen worktop height – between 85-95cm/40"-42" – depending on how tall you are. Bending too much will cause back problems, so consider raising your table/work bench on bricks or wooden blocks. Alternatively, scope out building supplies stores for adjustable height trestles.

Working surfaces can be made from a range of materials – ideally something that won't warp or bend and isn't too heavy for you to lift on your own. The print benches in our new studio are made from 2cm thick, dense foam, laminated in between two thin sheets of painted aluminium. Supported by adjustable height trestles, they're light, strong enough to stand on and guaranteed not to warp. One side has dense, 6mm thick industrial polyester felt glued to it whilst the other side remains as is. This means the work surface can be flipped for use as a normal table for dry work such as machine stitching. A hollow-form door, placed on trestles is a great option as it's light and everything can be dismantled and stored. Otherwise, use:

- 9 or 12mm plywood or MDF
- insulation foam – although this can crack if un-supported, so use it on top of a table top, or on trestles with a supporting board or planks.

Cover the work surface with two layers of acrylic/craft felt – stretched around the edge and stapled at the back to secure it. Two layers of old blanket or even a layer of old-fashioned carpet underlay/padding is also a good option but either way, avoid a consistency that's too soft/spongy. If you're creating a dedicated space/studio, make a work surface as large as the space will allow - you'll never regret having a decent-sized area to play on.

For most of our wet processes we cover the padded work surface with a drop cloth; heavy cotton drill or broadcloth are good options as they're thick and last for ages. The job of the drop cloth is to absorb excess wet media, prevent bleeding and protect your felt covering from becoming damp and contaminated with media.

In time, the drop cloths will become works of art in their own right – a great base for stitch, embellishment or printing.

Mike Wallace used simple tools to create an elegant background

Tools & Materials

As this book is about exploring different marks directly on to cloth, the range of tools you could use are almost limitless. We've gone into detail on six methods and broadly outlined how to approach found objects:

1. Scrapers, such as old credit cards or spreaders
2. Needle-nose bottles
3. Mono printing plates (smooth sheet plastic and acrylic plate)
4. A variety of brushes
5. Rollers of different types
6. Spray bottles / plant misters
7. Found objects: e.g. plastic grass doormats, packaging materials, cookie cutters and so forth.

In addition to these tools, you're going to need some other stuff:

- work surface, covered with the drop cloth, as described on page 4
- lidded plastic container for storing print paste (the size will depend on how much you make)
- bucket for mixing chemical water and a lidded container to store it in (plastic water bottles are fine)
- 6 to 10 spoons (we prefer metal to plastic as they don't snap). Have a selection of both teaspoons and dessert spoons.
- measuring spoons (teaspoons and tablespoons are the key measures)
- measuring jug (1 or 2 litre capacity)
- 2 metres/yards of sturdy sheet plastic
- lidded plastic containers for storing thickened dye paints or discharge paste
- some small pots for colour mixing (old yoghurt pots will work fine although pots with lids are handy)
- masking tape (1" and 2")
- kitchen/paper towel
- ball-headed or T pins
- cat/kitten litter tray, or a kitchen tea-tray
- an old towel

All of the above should fit into a large plastic storage box, ready to assemble when you need it.

Media

All of the approaches in this book can be used with a variety of media — some are great for cloth, some are great for paper and some are great for both:

- *Fibre-reactive Mx thickened dye paints;* Mx dye paints are suitable for all natural fibres except wool and won't alter the hand of the fabric.
- *Discharge paste;* will remove colour from Mx dyed cloth, with the exception of Turquoise which is usually resistant to discharge processes. Commercially dyed black discharge fabric should work, but always test a sample first.
- *Fabric paints;* will work on any fibre – including synthetics - as they sit on the surface of the cloth and require no chemical reaction with it. They will stiffen the hand to a greater or lesser degree depending on how they're applied.
- *Temporary & permanent resists;* water-soluble P.V.A, flour paste, soy wax or matte medium etc.
- *Acrylic paints;* perfect for paper, these can also be used on cloth but will stiffen the hand more than fabric paints.
- *Gouache;* perfect for paper explorations but not suitable for fabric.

If you're using cloth, it may need to be prepared for dyes before use, and we provide more detailed information on this in the Media & Recipes section (pages 39 to 49).

To keep things manageable, we've focused on the use of dye paints in our descriptions, but feel free to use whatever works best for you.

Cloth

You'll need to think about the type of cloth you want to work on, which may be determined by how you're going to use it. If you're planning to use Mx dyes, you'll need to choose natural fibres such as cotton, linen, hemp, bamboo, silk and viscose/rayon. Mx dyes won't work on wool – even though it's a natural fibre. Guidance on how to prepare your cloth to receive the dyes is given on page 41.

If you're opting for fabric paints or acrylics, they'll work on natural and synthetic fibres so your range can expand to include cloth such as polyester or nylon. And as intimated above, feel free to work on paper if that's your discipline as all of the approaches in this book will yield great results.

Making Your Mark

Many of the approaches outlined in this section will require you to pin your cloth to your work table. This will stop it from moving as you scrape, write, doodle, stamp, roller, or print. Make sure the tension is fairly tight as the cloth will stretch as you apply the dye paint, and you may need to re-tension and pin at some stage during the process. If you're working on paper, then consider taping it to your work surface.

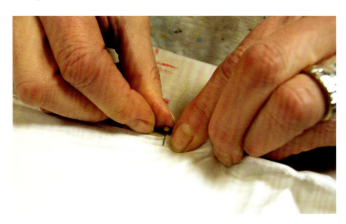

Scraping
Scraping is great for creating streaky marks and other visual texture. There are several scrapers you can use for this approach, including:

- old credit, membership or loyalty cards
- small squeegees or grouting tools with a smooth edge or rubber blade
- plastic paint scrapers

We prefer the first two as the lack of a handle seems to mean we engage more with the scraper – but try all of them and establish what works for you.

Choose a colour palette and remember if you go for a triadic colour scheme of three primaries, you'll get 'brown' at some stage if they're all mixed together. We recommend you undertake some samples before tackling a large piece of cloth. This will help you to get a feel for how you can alter the value and blend colours as you go along.

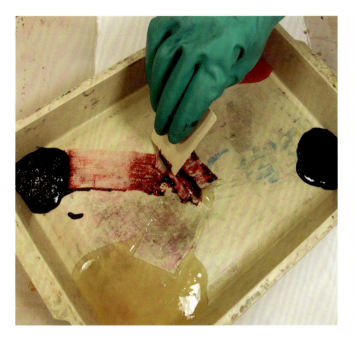

1. Our chosen weapon for this approach is a simple piece of plastic; an old credit, loyalty or debit card. It's small, lightweight, flexible, easy to use and generally costs nothing. You'll also need a plastic cat/kitten litter tray or tea tray; choose something that's not too deep.
2. Spoon a decent-sized blob of print paste into one corner of the tray and put your chosen colours in to the other corners. Keep the centre of the tray clear as a mixing area.
3. Using the plastic card, drag a small amount of colour out and then pick up a bit of print paste; roughly mix them, but not too much. Remember the greater the ratio of print paste to dye, the paler the value.
4. Scrape the mixture on to the cloth. If the paint and print paste mixture isn't well mixed, you'll generate visual texture in the form of streaky marks. Do this a couple of times, varying the load on the credit card as different quantities of media will generate different results.

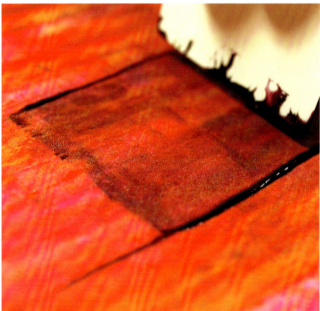

5. A heavily loaded card will create the main streaky mark, with fairly heavy lines either side of it.
6. These can be dragged out if desired, or left to generate additional texture.
7. A lightly loaded card will create the streaky mark, but with fainter lines either side. Again, these lines can be dragged out, or left for texture.
8. Now pick up a bit of one colour, and bit of another. Roughly mix them – or not; you'll get different results either way. Again, the amount of media loaded on to the card will effect the density of line either side of the scraped mark, which can be dragged out – or not.

9. Now play with directionality; keep scraping in one direction or…
10. Start varying the direction of your scrapes; vertical and horizontal and/or cross hatching.
11. Now try curves.

12. Or wiggly lines.
13. Maintaining the vertical can generate a sense of things rising or falling, or even suggest buildings or other forms.
14. Horizontal scraping can help you to build up strata of colour and value.
15. Experiment with short scrapes… and long scrapes.
16. Avoid too much over-lapping, or deliberately over-lap.

17. In addition to scraping, try using the edge or blade of the scraper as a stamp to generate line imagery – just dip the straight edge of the blade into a thin 'sausage' of dye paint and stamp with it. We also like to use strips of either 125 or 250 micron laminating plastic – laminated without paper in between - as it can be used straight or bent to produce lovely, thin lines.
18. Experiment with different types of cloth. A smooth, even weave will generate different results than cloth with literal texture e.g. something with a lumpy/bumpy weave.

A multitude of choices – it's very important to play and experiment when you start out. Pay attention to how you're using the scraper and the quality of mark you get. Work consciously and with a curious mind – this will enable you to develop control and mastery and in future, you'll know what to do to get what you want. Having used dye paints, try scraping with other media – particularly discharge paste – you'll get fabulous results.

'Little Bird', a work-in-progress by Leslie using various scrapers to drag and print

Writing, Doodling, Scribbling & Sketching

Most of us love the marks we generate on paper using pens, pencils, crayons and so forth and wish we could create something similar on cloth. Whilst there are options available, such as pens filled with fabric paints (some can be re-loaded, some can't), Soy Wax crayons or oil sticks, most of these preclude us from using dye paint, so we'd recommend trying a simple plastic squeeze bottle as a drawing or writing tool.

The image shows the options you have:

- Sauce or ketchup bottles; clear ones are best and these can be obtained from catering equipment suppliers. Avoid ones with caps - they get in the way.
- Needle-nose bottles; our favourites are plastic and we cut the tip of the nozzle to suit the weight of line we're seeking. Try sourcing them from textile, medical, chemical or laboratory suppliers.
- Silk painting bottles; these generally come with inter-changeable metal tips and can be obtained from textile suppliers.
- Re-loadable felt tips and rolling balls made by 'Montana' Markers.

The larger the bottles, the harder they can be to use. Our preference is a small size in soft plastic that's easy to squeeze without applying too much pressure.

These bottles can be used with a variety of media which may need to be adjusted to the right consistency. Ideally, you're looking for a consistency that pours off a spoon, rather than drops off it; something like single cream or runny honey – watch the DVD and you'll see what we mean. We've provided guidance on how to change consistency under each of the media sections, so do refer to these notes.

For the moment, let's assume you're using dye paint and have soda-soaked and dry cloth ready to go. Pin the cloth out on to the workbench. Make sure the tension is pretty tight as you don't want the cloth to ripple as you use the bottle. How you use the bottle will affect the end result:

- keeping the nozzle in contact with the cloth with generate finer lines.
- working with the nozzle off the cloth will lay down 'sausages' of paint which will gently spread and thicken.
- moving quickly will generate finer lines, moving slowly will generate fatter ones.

Bearing the above in mind, here's a couple of ways to proceed.

Writing

1. Make sure the nozzle of the bottle is running freely.
2. Place the tip of the nozzle in direct contact with the cloth (if you want fine lines).
3. Start writing – **we find it's easier to keep the nozzle in contact with the cloth and avoid squeezing the bottle too hard** – very little pressure is needed if the paint is the right consistency.
4. Try and work freely and let go of the need for things to look perfect. We observe that people set out to write neatly – as if they were back in school. Therein lies disaster! Let go, ignore the voice of your old teacher and just write – fast and energetically. If you have no idea what to say, write a stream of consciousness – whatever comes into your head. Don't worry if your lines aren't straight – if this matters, it'll either come with practise or you can rule your cloth with a chalk marker.

5. Write in swoops, curves, verticals, horizontals, wiggles – whatever. Just experiment.
6. Having covered the cloth with a layer of writing, let it dry out a little and then go back and write all over it again – layers of text can look fantastic as a background. You can stick to the same colour, or switch to a new colour.
7. Or, cure and rinse the cloth, iron it and then photocopy it on to acetate. You can then lay the acetate over the original cloth to get a feel for how multiple layers might look.

Doodling, Sketching & Dragging
Writing isn't the only option with the squeeze bottle:

Doodling or scribbling
Just go with the flow and what your hand wants to do. Do one layer, then another and maybe another.

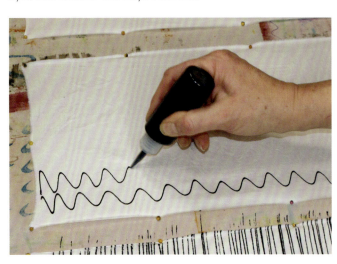

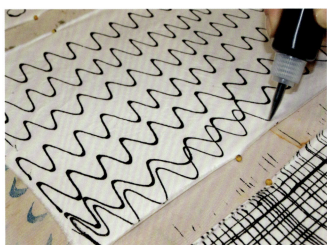

Sketching
Remember you're not in a drawing class. The bare essentials of form are often just perfect and if you do want to sketch beautifully, then go take a drawing class to learn better technique!

Dragging

Another approach involves drawing a thin sausage of dye on to the fabric and then using the edge of a credit card to drag it out. This will create a 'spine' of colour with raggedy edges. Or… write, doodle, scribble or sketch and then use a credit card to drag out the marks and colour the background. The dyes will have already started to strike, so you won't lose your original marks.

Whether writing, doodling or sketching (with or without dragging), consider working in layers:

- one colour in 3 values
- several colours laid on top of each other
- change direction
- change scale or weight of line
- combine straight and curvy

And whatever happens, remember that it'll take about 15 minutes for you to settle in so don't give up too quickly.

Mono Printing: Four Approaches

Traditionally, mono printing works by spreading an even coating of media onto a smooth, hard, flat surface (known as a 'plate') and making marks into that media using a variety of tools. Essentially, you're removing or pushing away an area of media to create anything from a fine line to a large shape, and this mark will then be reflected in the cloth (or on paper) as a negative image.

Once the plate has been prepared and marked, the cloth (dyed or un-dyed) is floated or rolled on to the plate and either gently patted down by hand or pressed down with a rubber roller or Brayer to pick up the media. It's then carefully lifted off, dried and processed accordingly. The label 'mono printing' is a result of only being able to make a single print from the prepared surface.

The 'plate' is traditionally made of glass, but we use either sheet acrylic or heavy, clear sheet plastic as it's cheaper, lighter, less likely to break and in the case of sheet plastic, can be stored rolled on a cardboard tube. The sheet plastic we use is clear - like glass - which is why we call it 'glassine'. It can be obtained from textile suppliers such as Jo-Ann (U.S.A.), stationery suppliers or good fabric shops. If you have difficulty finding it, use a white, smooth plastic tablecloth that can be easily wiped clean or hosed down.

We're going to cover four approaches to mono printing and we'll use thickened dye paint as our chosen media. Assemble the following:

- Approach 1: a large sheet of thick, smooth plastic or a smooth, white plastic tablecloth, big enough to cover your work table. Make sure it's un-creased.
- Approach 2: in addition to the sheet plastic, you'll need a selection of tools for mark-making. Choose a couple from the following options:

  - **Textured Rollers;** rolling pins with strips, stripes or other rubber shapes glued around the surface, sponge rollers cut to create pattern or with added rubber bands to indent pattern, decorating rollers with different surfaces.
  - **Drawing/etching tools;** anything that has a pen-like quality will enable you to draw into the surface of the media. These might include spatulas, ends of paintbrushes, tiling spreaders, wood grain effect tools, rubber massage or dog grooming mitts, cardboard of various textures, empty thread cones, tooth, shaving or pastry brushes, rubber sculpting 'shapers', old pens, plastic forks and knives, Afro combs etc..
  - **Lifting tools;** you can lift off media using plastic stencils, foam or rubber stamps, erasers, credit cards, spatulas, corks, grids such as non-slip rug underlay, sink protectors, plastic canvas etc.
  - **Masks;** once the required marks have been laid down, masks can be used to create windows or additional areas of interest; cut-out shapes from fine paper, found objects such as pressed flowers, leaves, doilies and fine laces can all be laid onto the surface between the media and the cloth, creating voids within the printed areas. When making your own cut-out masks, try to use fine paper as this will give you better results.

- Approach 3: a piece of smooth sheet plastic - not too thin and floppy – measuring 30x30cm (12"x12").
- Approach 4: a small, rigid piece of sheet acrylic or plastic. This can be any shape you like; square, rectangular, circular, triangular etc. You'll be using it like a stamp.

And for all four approaches you'll need:

- Foam and/or bristle brushes to apply the paint to the plate
- A rubber roller or Brayer for spreading the media out, and/or pressing the cloth down smoothly and evenly once laid on to the prepared plate.

You can use almost any wet media for mono printing but for crisp marks it needs to be fairly thick, sticky, reluctant to flow and able to retain it's shape on the surface of the plate. If you're using water-based paints (fabric paints, acrylics, gouache), acknowledge they can dry fairly quickly so you'll need to be prepared to work quite fast. Avoid working in a very hot room or in direct sunlight and always clean your tools and the plate as soon as you've finished using them. If you're in a rush, let tools sit in cold water until you're ready to wash up.

Almost any cloth is suitable for mono printing, depending on the effect you're looking for. Pre-dyed cloth that isn't up to scratch is often a good candidate for mono printing. Lurid commercials or hand-dyes can be subdued with the bright colours gleaming through the printed texture. Glitzy cloth can be made more subtle whilst still retaining its pizzazz. Dark cloth can be made richer with metallic paint or totally transformed through discharge.

The smoother the surface of the fabric, the crisper the marks and the more defined the images. However, textured cloth can be gorgeous as it tends to yield broken/fractured images or interruptions to the marks you've made. Corduroy, crinkled, pleated or wrinkled cloth can produce interesting effects. Experiment.

'Freefall/sloppy' mono printed and overdyed fabric by Turid Tonneson

Approach 1 - Freefall/Sloppy Mono Printing

This a slap-happy approach, frowned upon by purists. We love it as it generates great colour and generalised texture, which can act as a perfect base for other kinds of imagery. Our preference is to work both sides of the cloth and as you work, let go of your 'be perfect' driver.

1. Cover your workbench with smooth, thick sheet plastic/glassine.
2. Use masking tape to mark an area equivalent to the piece of cloth you'll be printing – there's no point in painting more of the plate than you need to.
3. Liberally squirt or spoon thickened dye paint on to the plate and spread it out using a foam brush, paintbrush or roller. Be aware that:

   - thick areas of dye will squelch and spread once the cloth is laid on top
   - thinner areas will be more ethereal
   - what you see on the plate is what you'll see on your cloth, but in reverse… so
   - keep working the dye paint until you're happy with the look of things.

4. Float your cloth on to the painted area of the plate and using your hand, gently smooth it down into the paint. Don't worry about wrinkles or creases – simply tug and pull at the cloth until it's smooth.

5. Lift the cloth off the plate and hang it somewhere.

6. Re-paint the plate and print the same side of the cloth, then hang it up and let it get almost dry.

7. Now repeat the process on the other side of the cloth, twice.

So, you've now mono printed the cloth four times: twice on each side. Hang it up to dry and don't panic! Things can look pretty messy at this stage, so let the cloth dry off a little and then decide whether to:

- Leave things alone; if so, roll the cloth in plastic to cure for at least 4 hours, and then rinse.
- Continue with more layers of mono printing; stick to the same colour, or add different colours. How many layers you undertake will depend on the amount of dye used at any given time. Do acknowledge that the soda ash present in the cloth can only handle a finite amount of dye. If in doubt, cure and rinse the cloth – you can always soda-soak it again and carry on with more layers.

This approach will generate cloth with general texture and varying depths of colour – a perfect background for additional layering. Working it from both sides will also give you a choice as to which side is the 'right' side. It can also be worth assembling a triple layer of cloth as a sandwich, hand or machine stitching it and then mono printing it. You'll get great effects as the paint will hit the ridges but won't get into the valleys created by the stitch line. This can be a great thing to do with fabric paint, as it's stiffer than dye paint.

Approach 2 - Mono Printing for Definite Marks

This technique requires a more considered approach, so we'd recommend you sample on smaller pieces of cloth to get an idea of the different effects you can get. Generally speaking, the more marks you make and the greater the number of layers of marks, the better the result, so try to vary your tools as you etch, draw or lift out the paint. Remember that any image you create on the prepared surface will be printed in reverse and if you don't like what you see, simply re-spread the paint and start over.

1. Cover your workbench with smooth, thick sheet plastic or if you're working on smaller samples, use an off-cut of sheet acrylic - about 30 x 60cm / 12" x 24" would be large enough.
2. Assemble your 'palette' of mark-making tools in a cat litter tray so they're close to hand.
3. Pre-prepare any masks you want to use. Remember that if you're making your own, cut the desired shapes/lines using fine paper (the finer the paper, the better the result).
4. Lay your cloth down on the clean plate and using masking tape, mark out the area you'll need to paint.
5. Using a piece of plastic pipe, roll up your cloth and leave it sitting on the roll just clear of the area you've marked out. DON''T pick it up, just roll it up and leave it as this will mean that once the plate has been painted and worked up, your cloth will be perfectly positioned to unroll across the painted plate.
6. Make a thickened dye paint in your colour choice – you can work in multiple colours later, once you've got the hang of things.
7. Liberally squirt or spoon thickened dye paint on to the plate and spread it out using a foam brush or rubber roller.

Be aware that:

- Too much paint can result in 'ploughed' areas as you shift and move the paint around.
- Too little means poor coverage; the marks may not be definite enough and the paint may dry too quickly.
- An even coverage of paint will generate the best results; not too thick, not too thin and evenly spread across the plate.

Make your marks using the tools of choice - watching the demo on the DVD will help you to get the idea and suggestions include...

8. Use shapers, tiling tools and the ends of pencils or brushes to draw, sketch, doodle, slash, dot, cross-hatch etc.

9. Use finer tools such as combs or door-mat plastic to blur the first layer and soften things up – or simply use fine tools in their own right.
10. Or, do the reverse; work finer lines first, then stronger ones. Fine marks will remain in the background when you apply stronger images/marks.
11. Use scraping tools such as old credit cards, bits of plastic or a spatula to lift out windows. Lifting out will often create a ridge of paint that can be dragged back into the window to create a ragged edge.

12. Use your pre-prepared masks to create windows as an alternative to scraping away the paint; simply lay the pieces of paper on top of the paint as a resist.

With this approach, you need to think about composition and the relationship and placement of the marks you're making. If you don't like what you've done, take a brush or roller and smooth out the paint before starting again – this is one of the joys of mono printing, you can have several attempts at getting something you like.

13. When you're satisfied with the effect you've created, un-roll your cloth across the painted surface. If you've forgotten to roll the cloth to one side, you'll have to float it down on top as best you can – or work with a friend to help you.
14. Gently smooth the surface of the cloth with your hands, or use the rubber roller. If you do see some creases/wrinkles, gently tug the cloth to get it flat. If the fabric is fine the media will bleed through, so take care not to smear it.

Lift the cloth off the plate and hang it up to dry out a little or lay it flat if there is risk of things running. Once things have dried off somewhat, roll the piece in plastic to cure for a minimum of 4 hours, and then rinse. Of course, once the first layer of monoprinting has dried out, there's nothing to stop you doing a second print on top of it should you choose to. As with most wet processes, the possibilities are almost endless…

- Use more than one colour of thickened dye on the plate.
- Work with damp fabric to generate bleed.
- Don't wash the plate after the first print. Simply apply a different colour and go at it again once the first print is dry.
- Print onto white fabric or pre-dyed fabric.

Approach 3 - Printing with Sheet Plastic

You may find large-scale mono printing challenging; painting and cleaning the plate is difficult, maybe the paint dries out too quickly or perhaps it's difficult to lay the cloth down smoothly. You get frustrated because you like the effect it gives and don't want the definite shape created by printing with small plates (see Approach 4). What to do? Use small'ish pieces of sheet plastic or glassine instead.

This approach works in a similar manner to the first method described – it's best for laying down colour and general texture rather than definite marks and will create a great background. You'll need:

- A piece of flexible, smooth sheet plastic or glassine, about 40cm/16" square (or any size or format you can manage… which'll be determined by the length of your reach!)
- Thickened dye paint or other media of choice
- A foam or painters' bristle brush, or a rubber roller to spread the paint.

To proceed:

1. Pin the soda-soaked and dry cloth on to the drop cloth.
2. Paint the sheet plastic with dye paint, but be careful NOT to work right out to the edges. Instead, feather the paint so it has a raggedy edge.

3. Press the painted plastic face down on the cloth.
4. Lift up the plate.

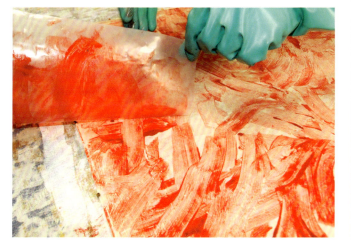

5. Re-paint the plate making sure it has a raggedy edge and lay it down so it slightly overlaps the first print.
6. The feathered-edges should mean you can blend all subsequent prints in a much more organic way, avoiding hard edges and obvious joins.

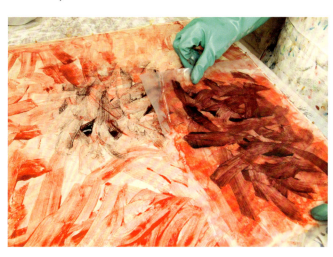

As before, you can work multiple layers in different colours, or simply build depth by printing multiple layers of a single colour. As always, you'll create something very textural, dynamic and personal.

A note on the positive image

And finally, remember that rather than paint the plate, you can sketch or doodle positive imagery on to it and print. The marks you make will spread or squish somewhat, but this can be very attractive.

Approach 4 - Printing with Small Rigid Plates

You can undertake either of the first two approaches using small rigid plates as stamping tools. This means you're taking the plate to the cloth, rather then the cloth to the plate. Most glaziers or sheet acrylic suppliers will have off-cuts they'll be happy to sell or give away. These can be cut to size/shape and used as stamping plates. Remember that the plate will print its own shape every time, so take a look to see what kind of shapes you can find in craft shops: circles (pot lids are a good alternative), ovals, stars, triangles etc.

Try looking in kitchen shops or hardware stores for small suction handles, as this will make the plate easier to use and avoid unwanted finger marks on the cloth. Failing that, glue a small piece of wooden dowel on to the plate to make a handle.

To use the plate:

1. Paint on the thickened dye with a foam or bristle brush or a roller – each will generate a different effect.

2. Experiment with the paint thickness; thick areas will blob and spread slightly whereas as thin layer will lay down very delicate traces. The choice is yours.
3. Use the plate as painted or etch marks into it with any of the mark-making tools discussed earlier.
4. Place the plate on the cloth and press.

5. Lift, re-paint and stamp until the cloth is covered to your liking.

Multiple layers of printing using a square of sheet acrylic (detail, Lucy Slykerman)

Variables include:

6. Working in vertical, horizontal or diagonal lines.
7. Straight lines are easier with a string guide: use pins to secure a length of cotton across the cloth, and follow the line. Once you've made your first line of mono prints, you won't need the string any more as you'll simply follow the line you have.
8. Work 'wonkily' varying the angle of the plate as you print.
9. Use several different colours.

10. Once you've done one layer, do another – going directly on top of the original prints or staggering them.
11. Apply paint generously to one plate, and then place another plate on top of it - squelching the paint. Prise them apart, which will generate squidgy marks, and you'll have both plates to take prints from.

This type of approach can either create a very structured look (particularly if you've 'tiled' your prints or worked in straight lines) or create an energetic look if you've worked randomly. Either way, you'll have made a great start to some personal cloth.

Making Your Mark | 21

Painting & Dry Brushing

The humble paintbrush is often a forgotten tool, but it's capable of generating fabulous colour fields. You have a few options available to you:

- foam brushes
- cheap house-painting bristle or acrylic brushes
- large brushes - try mops!
- artists' paintbrushes, Chinese calligraphy brushes and so forth

Let's take a look at some key approaches.

Painting & Colour Washing with Foam Brushes

Available from textile, art or decorating stores, foam brushes come in a variety of widths. Narrower widths are great for writing, sketching or laying down thinner bands of colour whilst wider brushes are great for creating colour fields.

You can work with liquid media, in which case expect a degree of bleed on the cloth – and this is something that can be exploited by working on wet, soda-soaked cloth, laid down on to plastic sheeting. You can also make more definite marks by working with thickened dye paint or do a Jackson Pollock by making a runny consistency suitable for dribbling, throwing and flicking.

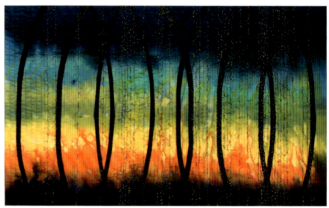

Janine Ayres worked wet-on-wet with liquid dye paint

1. Painting with liquid dyes and a foam brush will generate some bleed, but not as much as you might expect, depending on the humidity. Paint bands, loops, swirls, squiggles or plaids. Consider using a pipette instead of a paintbrush to drop the liquid dye on to the cloth.

Roger tries an alternative brush, much to the amusement of C Karen and Mezzie (photo taken at the Crow Barn, Ohio)

2. Use narrow brushes to sketch or write.
3. Use several colours or stick to a single colour but in several values.
4. Where different colours or values meet, expect some mingling but if you're working on dry cloth, also expect the line where they meet to be harder.
5. Work on damp cloth to increase bleed; simply spin out your soda soaked cloth and lay it out on to plastic sheeting and go to work.
6. Work wet-on-wet to encourage the dyes to really travel; soda soak your cloth and simply squeeze it out and lay it on smooth sheet plastic. The wetter the cloth, the more bleed you'll generate. This is a lovely way to blend colours and get interesting 'estuary' marks as the dyes travel across the cloth.
7. Having experimented with liquid dyes, move on to write, doodle or draw with foam brushes and thickened dyes. There'll be no real bleed to speak of and harder lines where colours meet. Work a single layer, let things dry out somewhat and then work another layer… and another.

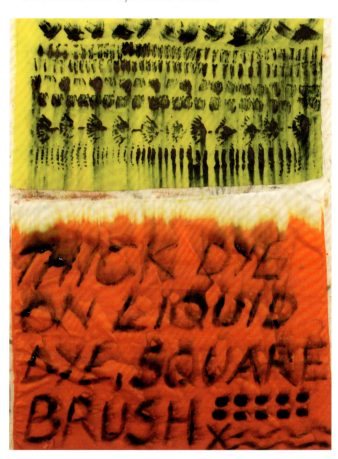

8. Finally, mix a runny honey or single cream consistency dye and try dribbling, spattering, flicking and throwing. You'll find you get different results depending on whether you work on dry, damp or wet cloth and whether the cloth is laid on to plastic (more bleed) or a drop cloth (less bleed as the drop cloth will take up excess moisture).
9. Try laying your cloth down on the floor (or the drive), and working it from above. Or, lean a foam core board against a wall and pin or clamp your cloth to it. If you do take this Jackson Pollock approach, work somewhere you don't mind making a mess and do acknowledge that the technique is harder than it looks!

Whatever approach you take, be aware of the following:

- the faster you apply the dye, the faster the cloth becomes wet… which means colours are more likely to blend and bleed into each other so…
- if working multiple layers you can choose to let the cloth dry out in between applications, or batch and rinse it before proceeding. If in doubt, batch and rinse as you'll understand what you have before deciding on your next move.

When finished, you have several choices:

- Leave the cloth flat on the workbench until it's almost dry – which may take as long as overnight, depending on humidity. Then, roll it in plastic and cure for at least 4 hours.
- Roll up the cloth in the plastic you've been working on and cure. Rolling when wet will encourage more blending and we've also been known to trample on the tube to really encourage this – but bag up the ends before you do this!
- Hang the cloth up; this will cause colours to drain from top to bottom. Keep an eye on the cloth if you do this, or you could end up with mud if you've used all three primaries! If hanging, we usually stand there and watch things unfold and when we're happy, we take the cloth down, roll it in plastic and cure it.

After curing, rinse well by hand and then machine.

Dry Brushing with House Brushes

House brushes come in a variety of widths and are easily and cheaply available from the DIY shop or hardware store. Our preference is bristle but you can opt for acrylic. We generally distress them before use by cutting into the length of the bristle – like a hairdresser making a fringe/bangs a little raggedy. We call these 'manky' brushes.

Whilst you can use them in a similar manner to foam brushes, our favourite technique is one we call 'dry brushing'. It's a slow, meditative process that generates streaky layers of colour. We find using 3 colours works well but you could use more once you've got the idea. You'll find the demo on the DVD useful, so read the guidance notes, watch the DVD then read the guidance notes again!

1. Mix Liquid Dye paints in 3 colours. For your first attempt we recommend you stick to the basic dye strength found in the recipe. You can choose to use paler values once you've got an idea of the potential end result.
2. Put each colour into a fairly shallow container, wide enough for the size of brush you're going to use (7 to 8cm / 3'' is a good width).
3. Have 3 brushes ready – one for each colour.
4. Cover your workbench with 3 drop cloths – things can get wet with this approach, so it makes sense to add extra layers of protection over your workbench.
5. Pin the dry, soda-soaked fabric under reasonable tension.
6. Start with the colour that's either going to be most easily adulterated by the others, or the colour you want to see more of.

7. Dip the brush into the Liquid Dye paint – don't saturate it, just get the tips of the bristles wet. Shake off any excess paint and starting off the cloth, gently sweep the brush across the cloth. Gripping the cloth and placing it under more tension will help to prevent rippling.

8. You need very little pressure. You're aiming for streaks of colour, not saturation. Try to keep the brush close to upright and use a light touch; just enough to make contact with the tips of the uneven bristles as you pass over the cloth.
9. Keep applying streaks of the same colour until you've worked your way over the entire piece of cloth.
10. If you're working a long length, you can move on to repeat the process with the second colour almost immediately. If working a small piece, let it get almost dry before applying the next layer. If the cloth gets too wet too quickly, the colours may bleed uncontrollably. The aim of this process is to lay down streaks of individual colour, which will mingle and blend where they meet.
11. Once again, let things dry out and then move on to apply the third colour.
12. Repeat steps 7 to 11, letting the liquid dye dry off in between passes.

Having applied two 'coats' of each colour (6 passes in total), review what you've got:

- *Have you got streaks?* If not, maybe you worked too wet and too quickly, so slow down a little and do something else in between passes.
- *Is one colour dominating?* If so, use it less frequently.
- *Is one colour being subdued or changed too quickly by the others?* If so, use it more frequently.
- *Do you need to introduce a fourth colour?* If so, mix the liquid dye paint and use it on subsequent passes.
- *Do you want to keep some white?* If so, you'll need maybe between 4 and 8 sweeps of each colour – 12 to 24 passes across the cloth in total.
- *Do you want to get rid of all of the white?* If so, either pre-dye the cloth to an appropriate colour in a pale value, or undertake many, many applications. Sometimes up to 20 passes of each colour are needed. If this is the case, consider curing and rinsing the cloth at the mid point, then assess it to gauge what colours to continue using, re-soda soak it, dry it and carry on.

As we said at the beginning, this technique is slow and meditative. We usually have something else on the go at the same time to allow the cloth time to dry out a little in between passes. We often leave the cloth overnight, sitting on the bench and carry on the next day, and possibly the day after.

The images and the demonstration on the DVD focus on straight sweeps of colour, but you can dry-brush in swoops and curves, work diagonally and create fantastic plaids by working horizontally and vertically. This process can create beautiful serene colour fields or striking, bold and energetic ones. The choice is yours, and experimentation will enable you to understand the possibilities.

Painting with Artists' Brushes

There are hundreds of brush types available across a broad price range. Start with brushes that are affordable and experiment before investing in anything pricey such as sable hair or Japanese/Chinese style calligraphy brushes.

How you hold, load and use brushes will make a big difference to the end result and we'd recommend devoting an entire day to experimentation. The picture below shows a variety of marks made with a single brush.

Curvy-linear dry-brushing by Pamela Niebauer

Rolling

There are a huge number of rollers to be found in craft shops, hardware stores & DIY stores. Just because they weren't manufactured for use on fabric doesn't mean you can't co-opt them. They're great for creating background texture and some can be used to make very specific and distinctive marks – you'll need to experiment with different rollers to find out what they can do.

A piece of sheet acrylic or an old vinyl tile works well as a plate for the roller – something rigid that doesn't bounce or sag will help you get better results… and here are some tips:

1. The material the roller is made of will make a big difference to the type of mark it can make, as well as how much media it'll pick up.

2. Sponge rollers may need some 'test drives' before they become sufficiently saturated with media to lay down a good mark.

3. If using a sponge roller, place a slim sausage of media at one end of your plate, and spread it out to load the roller.
4. If using a hard or decorative rubber roller, spread an even layer of dye paint on to the plate using a foam roller, and then pick up the dye paint with the rubber or hard roller – this approach will help to prevent blobby, uneven marks (although these can be interesting, so experiment).
5. Whatever type of roller you're using, check it to see it's well coated.
6. When using the roller, be aware that the pressure you exert will have an impact on the amount of paint transferred on to the cloth. Heavy pressure at the beginning of the roll will potentially cause splots and the roller is likely to run out of paint quickly. So, start with light pressure at the beginning and increase it as you progress. Re-load the plate and the roller with media as needed.

Variables include:

- Working in straight, curvy, or diagonal lines.
- Keeping to one direction, or working in many directions.
- Using a single colour but in several values.
- Using several colours.
- Working up layers or sticking to a single layer.

Having used the roller for the purpose it was intended, try generating other marks:

7. dip the roller in the media and stamp with it – this can create very interesting marks.
8. use the roller with with 'dabbing' motions instead of a rolling motion.

We find rolling can create skies, water and landscapes - including cities, deserts and forests. Until you've made some samples, you won't know what appeals to you, so be playful and experimental.

Spraying & Streaking

Spraying or streaking liquid dyes can become mildly addictive as you can cover a lot of ground quickly, but it's not for the faint-hearted. However, a degree of planning will help get the desired outcomes. Three options are available as tools:

- pump-spray bottles; usually sourced from textile suppliers
- plant misters; available from any cook-shop, hardware store or garden centre
- Squeeze bottles work best for strong streaks.

This approach works most effectively with several colours – but do be careful as uncontrolled blending may generate undesired colours. We also find that working on plastic gets the best results as the colours can bleed and blend more effectively – and damp cloth can help with this too. You can choose to work flat or vertically but do remember the dyes will travel quite quickly. If working vertically, you'll need to work quickly and keep an eye on things. To proceed:

1. Cover your work table with smooth sheet plastic, and lay down the cloth. Or…
2. Pin or clamp the plastic and the cloth to a piece of foam board and lean it against a wall (somewhere you don't mind messing up). Or…
3. On a still day, hang the plastic and cloth from a line, and use weights to keep it from flapping about. DON'T do this on a windy day or you'll end up with multi-coloured body parts.

4. Mix up 3 or 4 colours of Liquid Dye and transfer them to pump sprays or plant misters. Give some consideration as to where you want the colours and how much of each colour you want.
5. Start spraying: try to keep the mister upright as this will minimise drips but if drips do occur, wrap the bottle in a face flannel or piece of waste cloth.
6. Spray lines (straight, wriggly, curvy and in any direction), or shapes.
7. If the mister has an adjustable spray nozzle, set it to 'jet' and try writing, sketching or doodling.
8. Change colours as you wish.
9. If 'streaking', pour the liquid dyes straight from the squeeze bottle. Encourage more blending by spraying with more Liquid Dye or Chemical Water.
10. If working upright, be aware of how the dye is travelling and what effect this is causing. If you want to control the spread, work flat.

Roger and Jayne dribbling and spraying at the Crow Barn, Ohio

Roger has streaked the silk with liquid dyes and is encouraging blending by spraying with Chemical Water (image taken at the Crow Barn, Ohio)

Alternatively:

10. Do some mark-making or print imagery on the cloth in thickened dye paint and before it's dry…
11. Transfer it to plastic and spray it; you can achieve wonderful results where the thickened dye softens and runs into other areas – generally without losing its own integrity. Or…

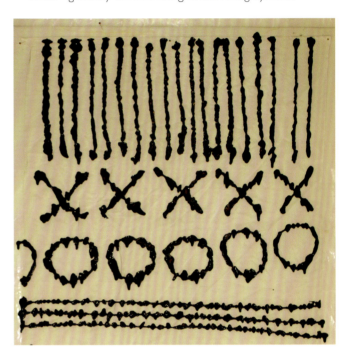

12. Spray the cloth, then print it or make marks – these will spread and bleed if you work wet-on-wet or you can choose to let the cloth dry out before adding more imagery.

When you're finished, either let the cloth dry out a little or simply roll it up in its plastic to cure before rinsing. Spraying can often generate 'one process wonders' – another reason it's addictive.

Using Found Objects

When travelling abroad, we love to visit new hardware stores, pet shops, cookware shops and supermarkets to find mark-making tools. We encourage you to be curious and have a least one attempt with free or inexpensive items. In terms of technique we find that:

- cat litter trays, tea trays and acrylic plates are best used as a palette from which to pick up the media
- stamping, dragging, dabbing, stippling and painting actions will generate different results with the same tool.

Faux grass/door matting

Made of green plastic 'grass', this is one of our favourite tools. Buy an entire doormat, cut it down and share it with friends. Plastic grass works best if glued to a wooden block as you've got more to grip. Great results can be achieved with stippling and dragging actions.

Cookie cutters

Most cook-shops sell metal cake molds and cookie cutters in a huge array of shapes - including letterforms and numbers. They work well with most thickened media and as long as they're made of metal, can also be used with Soy wax.

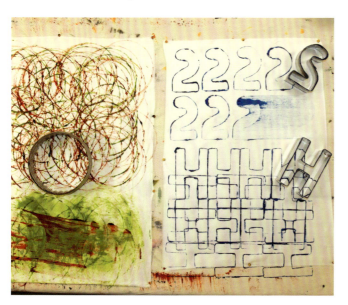

Alternative brushes

Washing-up, pastry and scrubbing brushes are great for large-scale textural marks. Silicone pastry brushes are delightfully wobbly and can be great for dribbling or spattering runny-honey consistency media on to cloth. Mops are great for loose, gestural marks.

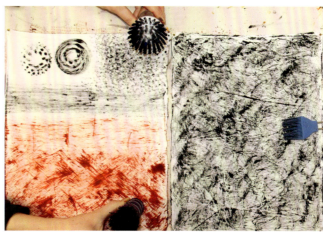

Pet grooming tools

If you don't own a dog or cat, get down to the pet shop anyway! The best grooming tools for textile use are those made of rubber rather than metal, as they won't snag on the cloth.

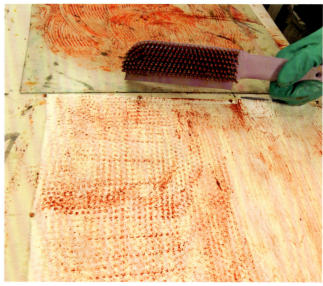

Making Your Mark | 29

Packaging materials

We all tend to get fed up with having to dispose of vast amounts of packaging but before you consign it to the bin or recycling box, check out how it works as a mark-making tool:

- *Corrugated cardboard:* most of us have plenty of this sitting in the recycling box. Cut it to size and shape and glue it to a plastic or wooden block, coat with PVA or Matte Medium and use as stamps. Or, simply use the edge as a stamping tool to create interesting linear marks.

- *Bubble wrap:* we use bubble wrap for making impressions when Breakdown Printing (see our book for detail on this screen printing approach), but it can also be used as a mono printing plate. It's available in different sizes of bubble and insulated swimming pool covers are also formed of a similar, but sturdier material:

   - cut it to any size or shape
   - using a foam brush, paint with thickened dye paint or other media
   - stamp or drag it on or across the cloth.

- *Foam & sponge:* both can come conveniently cut to a nice size or shape, or cut it to suit.

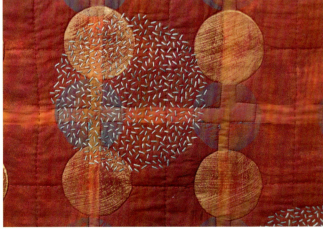

Daline Stott used a foam square to print in dye paints, then followed up with a pot lid using fabric paint

Mark-making by Sue Sheriff

- *Styrofoam and insulation foam:* we wouldn't recommend buying this stuff as both are environmentally unfriendly. However, sometimes it's unavoidable so if it turns up on your doorstep, use it before disposing of it:

    - use a Stanley knife and cut it to size/shape
    - consider using a hot knife/soldering iron to 'notch' or mess up the edges
    - use a hot knife/soldering iron to etch in designs
    - paint the media on, or create a stamp pad from sponge cleaning pads.

Note; if using a hot knife/soldering iron, work outside or in a well-ventilated area as there will be unpleasant fumes.

Scrap wood

Printing with scrap wood can be very rewarding particularly if the grain is strong or the wood has had bits chopped out of it.

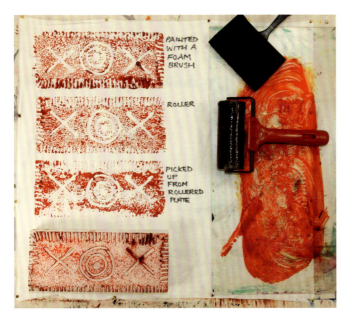

Scrunched-up baking parchment

Spread a thin layer of dye paint across a litter or tea tray and dab scrunched up baking parchment into it. Using a dabbing motion (don't press too hard), use the parchment as a stamping pad or stipple with it or drag it. Either way, you should generate great textural marks.

Making Your Mark | 31

Combining Approaches

Whilst we've covered each approach individually, there's nothing to stop you combining approaches and working up layers of different marks or textures. Take a look at the following images – the captions will tell you which approaches have been used.

Rollered, stamped with the edge of a foam brush, stamped with a credit card, over-dyed (Claire Benn)

Sketching with needle-nose bottle, scraping (Jayne Willoughby-Scott)

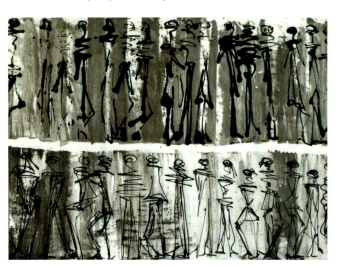

Top: positive image monoprinting, scraping. Bottom: sketching with a squeeze bottle, followed by scraping (both by Susan Chapman)

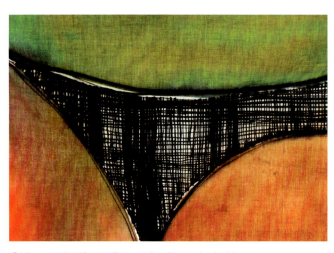

Grid created with needle-nose bottle, masked with soy wax, then sprayed (Jayne Willoughby-Scott)

Printed, sprayed, doodled and dripped (Lisa Sanderson)

Finding the Time

We'll all have too many ideas to execute in our lifetime. This can be a frustrating thought but try to console yourself with the knowledge that you'll undertake those you're meant to. But, we'd really like to encourage you to give the approaches in this book a try and to do this, you'll need to set aside some time.

We'd recommend you:

- Schedule time for yourself or it won't happen. Set yourself a schedule and diarise it. When you get a call with a request to baby-sit, go out to lunch, help with the decorating or take on some extra work you'll be able to truthfully say you have a previous commitment. No-one needs to know it's with yourself.
- If possible, allow an entire day for each approach. Whilst it'll take you longer to get to the 'finish line', it'll mean you won't feel rushed and have the opportunity to really explore and experiment. If this is too extreme for you, then spend at least 2 hours on each approach.
- Start by working on small scale pieces or samples as this will enable you to execute more ideas and give you a fantastic 'library' for future reference. We'd be the first to admit that we usually sample on a pretty large scale but most of the 'how to' images in this section were undertaken on pieces of cloth no larger than 50x50cm. Plus, if you hate some of the results, you won't have wasted money and time (and yes, we produced some real dogs when sampling for this book).
- Having completed all of the approaches, tear each sample in half, keeping a piece as a reference.
- Take the other half and add a second layer to it; stick to the same approach or choose a different one. Be guided by what you already have when choosing how to move on with the second layer.
- When these second layers are finished and processed, iron all of your samples and pin them up.
- Take time out to consider things. Make notes on what resonates or fits in with the kind of work you want to do. Make notes on ideas as to how to push each approach even further - it's unlikely you'll have exhausted all avenues.
- Make a decision as to where you'd like to start in terms of larger pieces, prioritise and then get going.

Ultimately, it's unlikely that using these approaches in isolation will get you where you want to be, but they'll make a great start. So let's now take a look at some of the things you'll need to consider to move work forward.

Susie Koren used a fine tjanting with soy wax on black cloth. The cloth was then discharged with bleach

What Next?

Your explorations into direct mark-making will have yielded some great cloth. What can you do with it? Some of it may be perfect for what you have in mind. Some of it will simply be background, so how can you move it 'beyond background'? Our book – **Finding your own Visual Language** (co-authored with Jane Dunnewold) - will give you a greater insight into composition and design, but generally speaking, you'll need to consider the overall composition of the piece. Pay particular attention to the 'figure-ground' - what's foreground (figure) and what's background (ground). This can be achieved by manipulating key elements to drive contrast:

- colour
- value
- imagery
- scale of imagery
- placement/balance

Ultimately, you're seeking to build contrast whilst driving relationship with what you already have. How you like to use your cloth will make a difference too, so let's look at this.

Wholecloth

There's much debate as to how any finished piece should be labelled. When we work with students we like to define 'wholecloth' as work made from a single piece of cloth, which might then be categorised as follows:

- *ArtCloth:* with artcloth, 99% of the compositional work is achieved through wet processes – similar to a painter working on a canvas. If stitch is added, its role is as accent. The work might be backed, stretched on to a canvas or hung as cloth but either way, the wet processes create the piece.

Claire Benn: scraping and needle-nose bottle (detail)

Discharged cloth, layered and stitched (Sara Heatherly)

- *Stitched Textiles:* a stitched textile may have more stitch than artcloth but the stitch doesn't significantly affect the composition. It may be there to define, to add literal texture or as an accent or feature, but the piece must be able to stand up compositionally without it.

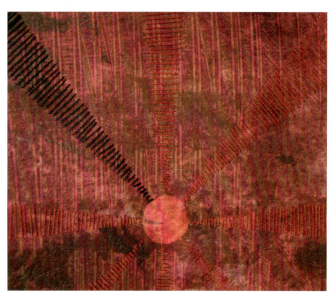

Claire Benn: monoprinting, hand-stitching (detail)

- *Wholecloth Art Quilts:* a wholecloth art quilt is a stitched textile with the addition of wadding/batting. The quilting may add to the overall finished look, but if the composition is poor, it won't be able to fix it.

Amelia Leigh: scraping, machine & hand stitching (detail)

Any wholecloth piece – with or without stitch – must work compositionally. If you're to go 'beyond background' in this manner you'll need to have the discipline to rinse, iron and contemplate the piece at almost every stage of process. Taking time out to contemplate how you're going to drive contrast and build relationship is part of making the work – even though it may not feel like it.

Embroidery

If you're an embroiderer, you're more likely to be making background cloth and going 'beyond background' with stitch. In other words, the embroidery will drive the strong compositional elements and the background is more of an 'underpainting' to provide the foundation for stitch.

Embroidered work by Jo Lovelock

Cutting Up & Re-Structuring

If you like to cut up and re-structure your cloth (e.g. collage or pieced quilts), the individual pieces of cloth you create don't need to work compositionally in their own right. You'll create the composition by the way you put them together. As such, consider creating a 'palette' containing:

- the colours you want to work in
- a range of values within those colours
- a selection of different 'patterned' fabrics – think about a range encompassing a variety of marks or textures (e.g. fine, organic, structured, graphic etc.)
- a 'feature' fabric that may have some kind of starring role.

And, acknowledge that once you start to cut and re-structure, you may need to return to the print table to create that missing element!

Detail of a stitched collage by Susie Koren

Garments

Great garment yardage can be created from any of the approaches in this book. It's highly possible you'll have something you can use but if things do need further accents or imagery, consider:

- *Scale;* avoid large-scale imagery as it can swamp the wearer.
- *Balance;* generally speaking, garment or interior yardage doesn't need strong compositional balance. You're likely to be going for a patterned effect.
- *Placement;* it can help to cut the pattern before working up the cloth. This will mean you don't inadvertently place a high-contrasting element on a sensitive spot – such as the groin or breast – or generate a target in the centre of the chest or back. You can also add accents on cuffs, lapels or along the bottom line of a jacket or shirt, or 'trail' elements up and around a skirt or dress.
- *Drape;* clothing doesn't sit flat on the body so consider draping the cloth on a design wall or pinning it to a garment dummy to see how this effects the look of things.

Leslie made the jacket and shirt by piecing various fabrics together

Interiors

Making cloth for interiors has some similarity to making cloth for garments. But, if you're seeking to make a roller or Roman blind consider that once dropped, it could act as an artwork. Plus, the size of the room or the drop of the curtain can allow you to use larger-scale imagery than you might with a garment, particularly if the viewing is at a reasonable distance. If you're making curtains, pin up the cloth twice - 'open' and 'closed' - to understand how the ripples will affect things.

If you're making upholstery fabric, be sure to drape it over a sofa or chair. For smaller-scale items such as cushions, use viewing 'L's to capture strong individual areas of the cloth. Then, cut the pieces to size (plus seam allowances) before you work on them further.

Cushions by Jo Lovelock

Reviewing & Auditioning

Whatever approach you take, regularly reviewing progress is vital. Even if you're working to a strong plan or vision do acknowledge that at times, a piece can take off in a different direction and you have to pay attention to that. If it's just been rinsed or had a hammering from stitch, press it to give it a chance to speak - this is particularly important with fibres that crease and crumple easily, such as fine silks or linen.

Then, get the work off the bench/table and place it as it will be seen. If it's for the wall, pin it to a design board. If it's for a garment, curtains or upholstery hang or drape accordingly. Then, take the time to sit and stare and make notes on what you see. Ask yourself:

- What does it have?
- What doesn't it have – what's missing?
- What colour(s), value(s), imagery, elements does it need?
- In what scale?
- Where do I place these elements in terms of balance?
- Am I on plan (if you have one) – can I proceed with next steps? Or…
- Do I need to re-think?

And if the piece is for the wall, always hang it in all four orientations. Whilst you may have set out to make a portrait piece, it may work better in landscape.

As you look, note down ideas as they come and don't stop to analyse them. Sometimes, when you stop to consider one idea you prevent the next one from coming in, so just keep going until you've no more ideas. Then look at each one and consider how it will move the piece forward. And that's the key question: "if I do X, how will it move the piece forward?". If you can't justify your plan, then it may not be a good idea to proceed with it.

To help you decide, try:

- *Photography*: take a photograph of the work and print 10 copies. Black and white prints will usually suffice and they'll also show you the value scale. Print 10 copies and use them to audition your ideas; draw, scribble, sketch, glue, cut and paste etc. Using photographs can be particularly valuable to determine how stitch can look, as the pen can mimic a stitch line.

- *The 'Dressing-Up' Box*: we keep a 'dressing up box' of fabric, paper and threads in the studio for students to dig about in. Sheers can be useful to see how the addition of colour or a darker value can work whilst allowing you to see what's underneath. Dense fabrics can mimic print or mark-making in dark values or show you what happens with the addition of elements such as a strong vertical or horizon line. Paper or fabric can be cut up into the type and scale of imagery you have in mind, and auditioned in different places.

Sheena auditions with fabric scraps

Acetates: you can draw shape, line or texture on to acetate to mimic further mark-making or print, and place it on your cloth without obscuring what's underneath.

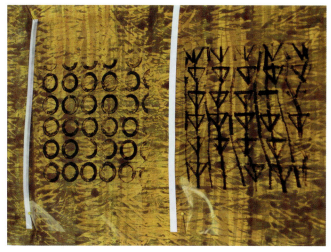

Whilst none of this will guarantee a successful outcome, it will give you an indication as to whether an idea has 'legs'. Ultimately there are no guarantees – you have to do the work to make the work. And remember, research states it take 10,000 hours (often spread over a period of 10 years) to develop true mastery. So when you're being hard on yourself, think about how much practice you've had. Developing mastery of any process takes time, effort, thought, application, experimentation and discipline. And it's fun, so enjoy the journey.

Media & Recipes

Procion-Type Mx Dyes

The basic list of 'ingredients' for using Mx dyes as paints is;

- Procion-type Mx Dyes
- Sodium Carbonate/Soda Ash (the fixative)
- Urea (a wetting agent)
- Anti-oxidant (Resist Salt L in the U.K. or Ludigol in the U.S.A. Available from textile suppliers)
- Water softener (Calgon from the supermarket in the U.K. or U.S.A, or use Metaphos from textile suppliers in the U.S.A.)
- Sodium Alginate for making print paste (we use Mantutex RS from Kemtex in the U.K. and ProThick SH from ProChem in the U.S.A.)
- A rinsing agent (such as Synthrapol or Metapex 38).

Suppliers of these ingredients can be found in the Resources section. And… don't get intimidated by this list of ingredients. If you can mix a gin and tonic and make soup or porridge you'll be fine.

Suitable Cloth for Mx Dyes

Procion-type Mx Dyes are formatted for use with natural fibres such as cotton, linen, hemp, bamboo, silk and viscose/rayon. They won't work on synthetic fibres such as nylon or polyester, nor are they effective with wool – even though wool is a natural fibre. Different fabrics also generate a different 'strike' or colour take-up. For example cellulose fibres (e.g. cotton) will take a dye colour differently to protein fibres (silk). Every type of cloth is different; some have fine fibres and others have heavy/thick fibres. Some are tightly woven whilst others have a loose weave structure. Let's take a brief look at this…

- *Fibre weight;* any type of individual fibre is only capable of holding so much dye. A fine fibre will hold less dye and fill more quickly, a thick fibre will hold more dye and take longer to saturate.
- *Weave structure;* a tightly woven fabric means the dye paint has to work harder to get inside the fibres, whereas a loose weave is easier.
- *Texture;* textured fabrics with slubs, ridges or accentuated weaves will break up or fracture the marks, which can be fabulous.

Note; we personally avoid using calico/muslin or other 'loomstate' fabrics for anything other than high-water immersion dyeing as it tends to 'push back' the dyes. If you choose to use calico/muslin or loomstate for the projects in this book, scour it very, very well and accept that it will take many processes and perseverance to get a decent depth of colour – but when you do get it, it can be fabulously rich.

As you work with dyes and different fabrics, it's always worth experimenting and making notes on the differences in dye strikes and colours. This means you'll be able to prepare dye paints that are right for the cloth and the colour saturation you're looking for… and you'll waste less dye because your quantities will be more accurate.

Preparing the Cloth

Whilst some cloth is supplied 'PFD' (meaning it's prepared for dyeing), others may not be, particularly if bought from retailers or market stalls etc. If in doubt, scour your cloth to remove the size or dressing as they'll prevent the dyes from penetrating the fibres. The easiest method is to simply pre-wash your fabric at 60°C. Consider washing it twice if you think it has a lot of size in it. To guarantee removal of size, it helps to scour fabric with soda ash/sodium carbonate and a rinsing agent such as Synthrapol SP/Metapex 38. If you don't have a rinsing agent, use a laundry detergent instead:

- Load the fabric into the washing machine (don't over-fill)
- Sprinkle in 3 tablespoons of Soda Ash and a half teaspoon of rinsing agent for a full load of fabric (about 6 metres). The amount depends on the quantity and type of fabric.
- Wash at 50-60°C.
- Any shrinkage will also occur at this stage, which is useful.

Silk Organza   Cotton   Silk-Bamboo   Silk Noil   Linen

Detail of work by Cindy Kearney: soy wax resist, scraped with thickened dyes

The Role of the Dye

The Mx dyes are your colouring agents (sorry to be obvious!). They're classified as cold water dyes but are manufactured to be used between 50-80°F and will therefore need to be cured or 'batched' to aid striking. Sodium Carbonate (Soda Ash) is needed to fix the dyes and this can be put into the dyes or into the cloth. The dyes are at their most dangerous to health in their dry/powder state so wear a good quality mask when mixing significant quantities. Equally, wear gloves when handling the dyes and if they do get on your skin, don't use bleach to remove them. Instead, use a cleaner such as Reduran to get the worst off - the stains will fade after a couple of days.

We source our dyes from Kemtex Educational Supplies and the list below shows the names and numbers as used by Kemtex at the time of writing. We've also included the ProChem (U.S.A.) equivalents – although other suppliers such as Dharma (also U.S.A.) supply a great range too. As a colour range we recommend two sets of basic primaries; 3 cold and 3 warm. Black and Dark Brown have been included to use as colours in their own right or to help you generate complex or dirtied colours and to darken/enrich.

Rich/Warm Primaries	Energetic/Cold Primaries
Scarlet Red Mx-3G (ProChem Mixing Red 305)	Magenta Red Mx-8B (ProChem Strongest Red 312N)
Royal Blue Mx-R (ProChem Mixing Blue 402c)	Bright Turquoise Mx-G (ProChem Turquoise 410)
Golden Yellow Mx-3R (ProChem Golden Yellow 104)	Acid Lemon Mx-8G (ProChem Sun Yellow 108)
Black Mx-K (ProChem Deep Black 609)	
Dark Brown Mx-3G (ProChem Chocolate Brown 511A)	

These eight colours will provide you with endless possibilities but feel free to invest in a larger colour range. It's also worth getting to know one supplier's products as the colours from each manufacturer will be different.

How much dye to use is a tricky subject. Colour is subjective and different weights and types of cloth will respond differently to the same mixture of dye paint. Another key consideration is that some colours 'strike' faster and more aggressively than others. For example, we find that Magenta (cold red) is the fastest striker, whilst blues tend to be slow. Undertake specific experiments using our recipes as a starting point and adapt them to suit.

The Role of Soda Ash/Sodium Carbonate

Sodium Carbonate or Soda Ash is the fixative used for the dyes. It must be 100% pure and can be sourced from many of the companies listed in the Resources section. We opt to buy ours in bulk from a swimming pool supplies wholesaler and if you do this, make sure the sodium carbonate is 100% pure and hasn't had chlorine added to it.

Once soda ash is added to a dye paint, the paint must be used within 4 to 8 hours. As such, we prefer to put the Soda Ash into our cloth, rather than our dyes as this means the dye paints will last – if kept cool – for about 4 weeks. We have a soda 'vat' on the go at all times so it's ready when we want to soak cloth. If kept in a lidded bucket, the solution won't evaporate or go off. Wear a mask when mixing significant quantities of soda as the fine particles are hazardous if inhaled. Wear gloves when coming into contact with soda solution otherwise you could develop an intolerance to it. This is the recipe we use:

- *3 tablespoons of soda ash per litre of water.* So, for a 10 litre quantity…
- use 450ml/g of soda ash in 10 litres of water or…
- use 225ml/g in 5 litres of water if this is a better quantity for you at home.

Soda Ash doesn't like being dissolved in hot water, so start by putting the required amount of soda ash in a bucket, add tepid water to get it dissolving an then switch to cold water to the desired volume. Store covered and it won't evaporate or go off.

- Put your dry or damp (but not soaking wet) cloth in your soda-soaking tub and leave for between 10 and 20 minutes.
- Wring out/spin and work with it wet (more bleed) or wring/spin and line dry to work with it dry (crisper marks).
- If you have a stand-alone spin-dryer, collect the run-off soda solution and re-use it.
- We avoid tumble-drying soda-soaked fabric for several reasons: a residue of soda is left behind on the drum; as the cloth dries, dry particles of soda ash are released into the air and can be inhaled; the effect of heat with soda may damage the cloth. Three good reasons to avoid the tumble dryer.
- Soda-soaked fabric can be stored for later use, but must be bone-dry. Silk will store for about a month whilst cellulose cloth can be kept indefinitely. **Note;** don't store your dry, soda-soaked cloth folded as it can generate a hard grid when you come to work on it - just stuff it into a bag or a box.

Chemical Water

Chemical Water is the starting point for all dye paints, so let's take a look at the 3 chemicals/agents commonly used to make it;

- Urea is a hydroscopic or wetting agent that stops the dye paints from drying out too quickly. The quantity needed depends on environmental conditions; high humidity will require less Urea and in extreme cases, no Urea. Very dry, arid conditions may require double the amount of Urea specified in our recipe. Please adapt the recipe to suit the conditions you're working in. We buy Urea in 25kg sacks from a local Farm/Feed supplier but it's available in small or large quantities from textile suppliers. Try to keep it dry to avoid lumping.
- A water softener such as Calgon (or Metaphos) is necessary if the water is hard as this can affect colour strike.
- An anti-oxidant such as Ludigol, Resist Salt L or ProChem Flakes is useful where air or water pollution may affect the dye colours.

Whatever combination of ingredients you end up using, chemical water is easy to make (think mixing a very large G&T) and convenient to have ready to hand. Stored cool, it will keep indefinitely and volume quantities are:

Warm Water	Urea	Ludigol	Calgon
5 litres	500ml / 400-500g	25ml	25ml
10 litres	1000ml / 800-900g	50ml	50ml

As a rough guide, 50ml Urea = 35g weighed.

In hot, dry weather, increase the quantity of Urea by approximately 15-20% to prevent the dye paints drying out too quickly.

In humid/damp conditions, reduce the amount of Urea to prevent the dye paints becoming too runny.

Dye can be mixed into chemical water to create liquid dye paints, but more on this later.

Print Paste

To make print paste, a thickening agent - Sodium Alginate - is added to the Chemical Water. In the UK we use Manutex RS from Kemtex. When working in the U.S.A, we use ProThick SH from ProChem. Dye is added to this paste mixture to create a consistency that's suitable for screen printing and many other direct surface applications.

We usually make about 4 litres at a time and keep it in the fridge, where it will last for about 4 weeks. If you've got some that's been hanging around for longer it may smell of ammonia and have gone off, so throw it away.

However much you make at a time, you can mix by hand, use an old food processor or better still, a hand-held electric stick blender. We mix a thicker-than-usual print paste that has a 'dropping' rather than a running consistency as it's more suitable for processes such as Breakdown Printing, and can be easily thinned by beating more Chemical Water into it. If you can make soup or porridge, making print paste is easy so here are recipes for three different quantities:

Chemical Water	Sodium Alginate Manutex RS/ProThick SH
1 litre	45ml / 30-35g
2 litres	90ml / 65-70g
4 litres	190ml / 130g

If mixing by hand or with a stick blender, put the required amount of Chemical Water into a tub, start mixing and slowly sprinkle on the Sodium Alginate as you mix. Mix thoroughly for about 2 minutes and then leave in a cool place for at least 4 hours to thicken up, ideally overnight.

Making Dye Paints

As mentioned, we generally prefer to put the soda in the fabric rather than in the dyes. There are several reasons for this;

- The dyes last longer as there's no soda for them to bond with.
- We've observed that thermofaxes can break down more quickly when used with dyes that have soda in them. We suspect this is down to the soda; the repeated pulling of soda-dyes seems to set up an abrasive reaction that breaks down the plastic coating on the mesh.
- Processes such as 'Breakdown Printing' need dyes without soda in them, as the prepared screens will often take all day to dry.

When creating cloth where elements of white are important, you may want to switch to the soda-in-dye method. It can be hard to keep white areas pure even with ice-cold rinsing, particularly when Magenta dye is present. Soda-in-dye means that the areas of white cloth you've left un-touched have no soda in them, so staining is less likely.

Different Mx dye colours strike more quickly and more aggressively than others. We tend to compensate for this when making dye paints by using 'skinny' or 'fat' teaspoons. For example, reds and yellows (and therefore oranges) generally strike more quickly than blues and blacks…

Black; when mixing black, you may want to consider doubling the dye quantity to get a 'true' black.
Turquoise; a slow striker, so consider increasing the amount of dye by half or using 'fat' measures to help it keep up with faster bed-fellows.
Yellow; when mixing yellow, consider increasing the quantity by half or using a 'fat' measure. Whilst it strikes fairly quickly, yellow is easily contaminated by other colours. You may need to keep larger quantities of yellow as it tends to get used up more quickly.
Magenta; the fastest, most aggressive striker of them all, consider using 'skinny' measures.

How much dye you put into your paint mixture is very personal as we all describe the depth of any colour differently. Equally, the type of fabric will determine the colour strength; fine silk fibres need less dye than heavier cottons and linens. Generally speaking, the more dye used, the more intense the colour. A good starting point is to mix up a fairly strong mixture and reduce the colour strength as you need to by adding more Print Paste or Chemical Water. Our recipe will make a quarter-litre (250ml - about 8 fl oz) of paint. Dyes in our studio are always mixed to this recipe/strength, and weakened as required.

> **TO MIX DYE PAINTS**
> - Put a little warm water in a container twice the size of the volume of paint you're making; you'll be stirring vigorously.
> - Add 2 teaspoons of Mx dye powder and stir well to dissolve.
> - Now top up to 250ml / 8 fl oz with Print Paste to make a thickened dye paint, beating the mixture well until it's smooth or…
> - Top up to 250ml with Chemical Water to make a Liquid dye paint.

1. Dissolve the dye

2. Top up with print paste to make thickened dye, or…

3. Top up with Chemical Water to make Liquid Dye

We store our thickened dyes in twist-top ketchup bottles but these are almost impossible to find now. A good alternative is clear, polypropylene sauce bottles obtained from catering equipment suppliers. Our liquid dyes are either kept in the same sauce bottles or plastic screw-top bottles. Mx dyes will gradually bond with water at warmer temperatures, so their shelf life is limited once mixed. Shelf life can be prolonged by keeping the mixtures in the fridge (covered), but it can be risky to use them after 4 weeks and there's no guarantee on results.

So, you now have four types of media at your fingertips:

- Chemical Water
- Liquid Dye Paint
- Print Paste
- Thickened Dye Paint

These four things will enable you to mix any colour you want, any value you want and any consistency you want. Let's explore how.

Colour Mixing

Colour mixing is best learned by experience – mixing colours together in different proportions and observing the results. As a starting point, note that mixing energetic, cold colours together will generate different results to mixing rich, warm colours together. For example;

- Lemon Yellow & Magenta will give you a bright, brilliant, 'acid' orange whereas…
- Golden Yellow & Scarlet will give you a warm, rich orange.

- Lemon Yellow and Turquoise will make a brilliant, sparky emerald green whereas…
- Golden Yellow & Royal Blue will give you a dirty green - not quite olive, but almost.

- Turquoise & Magenta will give you a bright, sparky purple whereas…
- Royal Blue & Scarlet will give you a plummy purple.

Ultimately, the best way to learn about colour and colour mixing is to get stuck in with the dyes. The first rule of thumb is never assume the way a colour looks in the pot or when wet on the fabric is the way it'll look once rinsed and dried. Always assess the colour on a piece of paper towel first – whilst this won't be totally reliable (paper towel isn't cloth), it'll give you an indication. As you work, consider keeping a dye notebook to record the colours used, in what proportions and combinations. Equally, tear off little bits of cloth from your experiments and glue them into this reference book, which will give you a truer record of the way the different mixtures work.

Think about what colours you're trying to achieve. Are you looking for, bright, high-energy colours? If so, explore the energetic, cold primaries. Are you looking for rich, muted, warm colours? If so, explore the rich, warm primaries. Then try mixing energetic colours with rich colours to find out what else you can achieve.

And then there are the 'complex' colours. We define a complex colour as a colour that's been adulterated to make a 'dirtier' version of itself. The key principle for making any colour more complex is to use a small amount of its complementary colour. The complementary 'couplings' are:

Primary Colour	Complementary
Red	Green
Yellow	Purple
Blue	Orange
Secondary Colour	**Complementary**
Green	Red
Purple	Yellow
Orange	Blue

For example:

- to mix a complex primary (say ochre), start with Golden Yellow (warm yellow). Bit by bit, add purple until the golden yellow had turned to the ochre you see in your head. You could also choose to use Brown as the dirtying agent, so try different approaches.
- to mix a complex secondary (say rust orange), start by mixing an orange from equal parts of golden yellow and scarlet, and then add blue bit by bit until you get the rust orange you're seeking.

It's all about the proportions of the colours used. As a basic guide we'd recommend starting with 1 part of the main colour (e.g. orange) and then adding a tenth part (10%) of the complementary (e.g. blue). Our 10%'s aren't precise and may not be enough, but you can always add more – bit by bit – until you get what you want. This is easier than adding too much at the beginning and having to correct.

Some of our other books – such as **'Screen Printing'** and **'Thermofax Printing'** – have sections dedicated to colour mixing and offer lots of recipes, so if you need more help, consider investing in them.

Changing Value (making things paler)

We recommend making your 'stock' dye paints fairly strong as it's much easier to make a dark paint paler than make a (too) pale paint darker. In simple terms, to reduce the value of a colour, simply increase the proportion of 'base' to dye quantity as follows:

- For Liquid Dyes; add more Chemical Water and stir well
- For Thickened Dyes; add more Print Paste and beat well.

The greater the proportion of chemical water/print paste to dye, the weaker the value and to achieve a tint, you may need to go as high as 1 part Thickened or Liquid Dye to 20 parts Print Paste or Chemical Water.

Changing Consistency (making things runnier)
For some of the approaches in this book – such as needle-nose bottles - you'll need a consistency that's somewhere between liquid and thickened. When changing consistency, it's generally easier to make a Thickened Dye runnier than a Liquid Dye thicker.

So, to change consistency and maintain the strength or value of a primary colour:

- add liquid dye to thickened dye until the consistency is as you want it.
- be aware that for most of the approaches in the book, the thickened dye doesn't need an equal amount of liquid dye to make it the consistency you need - generally speaking, you'll use less Liquid than Thickened.

To make a runny secondary colour, you may have to experiment a bit depending on the exact type of secondary you need:

- using thickened dye, put the key primary colour in a mixing beaker; let's say it's yellow.
- to make runny green, add liquid blue dye until you get the consistency and colour you want.

Sometimes, the consistency can be right, but the secondary isn't quite where you want it to be. If this is the case, you may need to:

- mix the secondary colour in both liquid and thickened dye
- add the liquid version to the thickened version until you have the consistency you want.

Either way, beat the mixtures well to get rid of lumps. When making runny mixtures, we usually use a small jug – the best ones are those with fine spouts and these often come free with new irons. A jug with a nice spout will make it easier to pour the mixture into a needle-nose bottle or similar. If you can't find a suitable jug, make the mixture in a pot and use a syringe to transfer it.

Changing Value & Consistency (paler & runnier)
At times you'll want to make the dye paler and runnier. You can achieve this in one of two ways, depending on the value you're seeking, and the consistency you're seeking:

- add Chemical Water to Thickened Dye. Beat well until you have the consistency you want. Normally, you don't need equal proportions to get the right consistency, so if you've got the right consistency but the value is too dark…
- you'll need to keep adding a combination of print paste and chemical water until you get what you want.

Curing/Batching Thickened Dye Paints

In addition to soda ash (which is already in the cloth, or the dye paint), three other 'ingredients' or conditions are required to maximise the dye/fibre reaction:

Moisture:	Almost dry to the touch or very wet
Heat:	15°C - 35°C (60°F - 85°F)
Time:	4 hours as a minimum, overnight or up to 24 hours

This process is often referred to as curing or batching.

Moisture
Dye molecules can penetrate fibre more effectively when moisture is present, although the amount of moisture can be so little that the fabric can feel almost dry to the touch. If the fabric has dried out very quickly or feels bone dry to the touch, the reaction will stop, so avoid drying fabric in direct sunlight, drying it too much or too quickly. You can retain moisture content by using plastic sheeting (cover the fabric with it or roll it up). We prefer to let pieces dry off a little before rolling in plastic, as we hate washing plastic! If your cloth does get too dry and you're worried about a good strike, lay it on plastic and re-hydrate it by spraying lightly with Chemical Water. Then roll it up.

Heat
Cure between 15°C - 35°C (60°F - 85°F). If the temperature's too cold, the reaction of the dye is slowed down or even halted completely. Too hot and it may dry too quickly for proper curing.

In the summer or if the studio is heated overnight, let the cloth sit there, curing gradually in or under plastic. In winter or in an un-heated studio, roll it up in plastic sheeting (very wet or almost-dry) before sliding the tubes in between a folded electric blanket, set to the highest temperature to provide even background heat. If you can't get hold of an old electric blanket, place the bundles somewhere warm – under (but not on top of) a radiator, on a heated floor, over an Aga/stove or near a boiler - and cure for a longer period.

You can put the rolled cloth in direct sunlight to batch, but always cover it with black plastic as U.V. rays can react with the soda ash and generate uneven strikes.

Rolling when wet may cause colours to bleed and blend, which can be fantastic. If you want to keep colours separate or keep the marks crisp, don't cover or roll when very wet - let the piece semi-dry then cover or roll in plastic before curing.

Time
Allow 4 hours as a minimum or ideally overnight for curing, as the dye needs time to react with the fibre molecules. Our standard curing time is 12-18 hours/overnight, and we find it exciting to get rinsing the next morning. If you can't get decent heat for the curing process, let things sit in plastic for 24 hours to give the dyes a better chance to strike.

Rinsing
If you can, use a rinsing agent such as Synthrapol/Metapex 38 as it will 'trap' dye particles and help prevent colour contamination. You'll need a few drops to a half teaspoon when hand-rinsing, and about a half teaspoon for a full load when machine washing – it all depends on the size of the load and the heaviness of the fibre. If you don't have a rinsing agent use a mild detergent suitable for delicates or woollens – just make sure it's pure and doesn't have chlorine or bleach added to it.

- Rinse off excess dye in **cold** water and a rinsing agent in a bucket, changing the water regularly.
- Change to hand-rinsing with hot water for several changes (be sure to use a rinsing agent when rinsing with hot water).
- Switch back and forth between hot and cold rinses several times, finishing with a cold rinse.
- When hand-rinsing, keep the cloth moving to prevent cross-printing. If you need to wait for the washing machine, leave the hand-rinsed fabric sitting in plenty of cold water to minimise cross-printing.
- Machine wash **cold** with a rinsing agent, once or possibly twice if an aggressive colour (e.g. Magenta) is present.
- Machine wash again in warm water with a rinsing agent at 40-60°C

If you wash in hot water too quickly, excess dye particles may transfer and cause staining to other fabrics (although the use of a rinsing agent will help to prevent this). Remember – the stronger the colours/the more dye you've used, the more washes you'll need. If we know we're taking the cloth on to another dye or discharge process involving more washing, we normally undertake a thorough hand rinsing process and then do a cold machine wash before proceeding with the next wet process.

Sometimes the sodium alginate/Manutex RS in the thick dye paints can be difficult to remove. This can happen if the dye paint has dried out too fast (e.g. the cloth has been hung to dry in direct sunlight). If so:

- dissolve 1-3 tablespoons of soda in hot (about 60°C) water. The amount of soda is dependent on the amount of cloth, but we find that 3 tablespoons handles a large piece of cloth.
- add a drop of rinsing agent.
- put the cloth into the bucket and give it a good mashing, then leave to soak for between 10 and 30 minutes, mashing occasionally.
- rinse out by hand in warm to hot water.
- do a final warm/hot (40-60°C) water rinse by machine.

If the sodium alginate/Manutex RS still hasn't shifted, repeat the process.

Some colours can seem to take forever to rinse out – reds are a good example. If you're worried you haven't got rid of all excess dye, soak the cloth overnight in a full bucket of cold water with some rinsing agent, then rinse it again in the machine at 40°C.

Claire scraped the cloth with dye paint, then scraped it with discharge paint before applying fabric paint using a credit card and lamination plastic

Discharge Paste

Discharge chemicals are used to remove dye colour from cloth. They won't work on all types of dyed fabrics, so testing is important. Turquoise Mx dye is usually resistant to discharge, so always test fabric containing turquoise.

Mx dyed cloth or commercial discharge cloth will normally discharge with one or all of the following, although each will discharge to a different colour:

- Jacquard or Dharma Discharge Paste: available ready-mixed but it can have a limited shelf life, so be cautious of buying in a lot of stock.
- Thiourea Dioxide (Thiox) powder/crystals: sold as Spectralite in the U.K., Thiox needs to be mixed with soda ash to activate it and has a limited shelf-life of about 4 hours.
- Formosul powder/crystals: this is our preferred discharge chemical. It's much cheaper than buying ready-made paste, requires no additional chemicals to activate it and will store for about 4 weeks if kept cool.

Formosul will discharge Mx dyed cellulose fibres and silk, but not wool. The powder will oxidise and lose strength when in contact with air, so decant into smaller tubs as you use it, or pack out the void in the container with bubble wrap or similar.

Formosul is activated by heat and steam and can be mixed with print paste, water or a combination of both to get different consistencies. Always work in a well-ventilated area and/or wear a good quality mask when handling the dry powder/crystals, and when steam ironing.

The basic ratio is 1 part Formosul to 10 parts 'carrier'; which can be water or Print Paste. This ratio makes a fairly strong solution, but its strength can be reduced by adding more water or print paste. To mix 500ml /16fl oz of paste:

- Dissolve 50g (3 generous tablespoons) of Formosul in a little warm (but not hot) water and dissolve.
- To make a paste: top up with 500ml of print paste and beat with a stick blender.
- To make a liquid: top up to 500ml with cold water.
- Store covered, in the fridge or somewhere cool.
- Liquid Formosul can be mixed with Formosul Paste to create runnier consistencies suitable for needle-nose bottles, painting, and spattering. Beat the mixture to make sure it's well combined.

Note; ProChem sell Formosul in crystal format and it needs to be dissolved overnight in a little water before use. Alternatively, wear a mask and grind the crystals into a powder using a pestle and mortar or an old, dedicated coffee grinder.

To use and activate Formosul:

- Pin out your dry, coloured cloth (it should not have been soda soaked).
- Apply the Formosul paste or liquid in your chosen manner then let it dry; hang it up or leave it on the bench if bleeding or running is likely to occur.
- When the Formosul is completely dry, use a steam iron set to cotton and maximum steam to activate it. The iron is a tool and the way you use it will effect the results you get; the more you steam the more the paste activates. The less you steam the less the paste activates. As such, you can achieve varying shades of discharge by using the iron creatively. Always work in a well-ventilated area and wear a suitable mask.
- Sun activation; you can also experiment by activating the paste with sunlight. Having applied the paste, position the piece in direct sunlight; as it dries it will slowly discharge. We've had great results using sunlight and it avoids the fumes. However, do test this approach as generally speaking, the colour and depth of discharge will be different. We tend not to activate heavier weights of cloth with sunlight as the light can't reach deep into the bulk of the fibre.

After activating by steam or sunlight, rinse the cloth by hand or machine. If the dried-in paste proves stubborn to remove, wash in hot water with some soda ash added to it.

Fabric Paints

There are many water-based paints available on the market. Here are a couple of pointers to help you understand the various choices:

- All fabric paints are related to acrylic paints. The difference lies in the formula of the paint. All acrylic and fabric paints have a binder, which is the polymer part. The colour comes from the addition of pigment - the pure colour. Fabric paints also tend to have softeners, surfactants (wetting agents) and other ingredients to make the paints more sheer and to reduce the impact on the hand of the fabric. This is easily tested; just paint or print a piece of fabric using an acrylic paint then paint another small sample of cloth using a good quality fabric paint; nine times out of ten, the acrylic paint will dry to a stiffer hand.
- Both are water-based pigment products that coat the surface of the fabric rather than penetrating and reacting with it (as in the case of Procion-type MX dyes). As such, they're suitable for use with both natural and synthetic fibres.
- Textile 'screen inks' are another name for printable fabric paints. They usually contain a drying retardant to reduce the potential of the paint drying in your screen, and sealing the mesh.
- Both are very light fast, far more so than Mx dyes. Data sheets showing the performance of different colours are available from most manufacturers.

A simple way of looking at these polymer paint products is to consider two key continuums:

Consistency		
Liquid	←——→	Heavy body
Transparency		
Transparent	←——→	Opaque

Generally speaking, the C2C studio uses printable consistency, transparent/translucent paints, although metallics veer towards the opaque as the sparkly mica also creates a level of opacity.

General Guidelines

- Different brands and types can usually be mixed together to create different levels of translucency or consistency, but do test how well different brands react to each other.
- Metallics can also be mixed with ordinary colours to generate lustrous effects.
- Fabric paint will stiffen the hand of the fabric but often, the hand is returned back to normal after washing.
- If you use Mx dyes on cloth subsequent to using fabric paints, the integrity of the paint colour will depend on the opacity of the fabric paint; sheer or transparent colours will be affected the most. It can be very rewarding to use fabric paints (or even a clear medium such as Matte Medium) to act as a permanent resist.
- Do not use fabric paints on cloth that has been pre-soaked in soda.
- Work on ironed or un-ironed fabric; un-ironed can create nice texture, but iron first if you want a smooth, crisp result.
- Work on dry fabric, wet-on-wet or wet-on-damp. Working wet-on-wet can achieve great results but in a similar manner to dye, the true results may not be apparent until the paint has settled into the cloth and is dry.

- Apply them using the usual surface application techniques (painting, dragging, stamping, monoprinting, screen or thermofax printing etc.)
- Wash up your tools immediately. If fabric paints dry out in your tools, they'll be ruined.
- You can build up layers of fabric paint without heat-setting each layer.
- Hang work in direct sunlight for fast drying… but never use fabric paints in direct sunlight as they may dry out in your tools and ruin them.

Altering Consistency & Transparency
As with dye paints, you can alter both the consistency and transparency of your fabric paints.

- To alter transparency; add transparent extender base to heavy-body paints and add water to liquid fabric paints. You'll need to experiment with proportions until you get the transparency you want.
- To alter consistency without changing transparency; add liquid fabric paint to heavy-body paint until it's as runny as you need.
- To alter consistency & transparency; add water to heavy-body paints.

Beat all mixtures well and get rid of any lumps.

Heat Setting
It's always a good idea to follow the manufacturers' instructions, but generally speaking, the following principles apply:

- Once the paint has been applied and dried, 'air-cure' for 24 hours before heat setting (in other words, hang the work to let the air flow around it). This will allow the paint to form a more effective bond with the surface of the cloth.
- All fabric paints require heat-setting if they're to be washed, and we always heat set even if the piece is unlikely to be washed. To heat-set, simply iron the cloth using parchment and a dry iron, set to somewhere between the wool and cotton setting.
- Work with the fabric right side up, using a pressing cloth or baking parchment to avoid paint/ink transfer onto the iron and to prevent scorching. Whilst we all hate ironing, don't skimp – follow the manufacturers' instructions on timing and iron settings. We usually flip the cloth over and repeat the process from the back (belt and braces!).

Once the fabric paint has been set, your fabric can be washed, but this isn't a pre-requisite. We don't normally wash until about a week after heat-setting to really allow the paint to settle. Often, any stiffening of the hand of the cloth is returned back to normal after washing. One point worth noting is fabric paint that's stitched and then un-picked will leave holes that won't close (even with washing), which could be a feature – or not.

Using Resists
Any of the approaches in this book can be used in conjunction with resists. These can be applied at any stage in terms of layering; before or in-between processes. Resists could include:

- masking tape
- book-cover plastic/cover film
- freezer paper
- string, paper, lace etc. – this kind of resist won't work with all approaches but can be very useful when mono printing
- soy wax; a great alternative to Batik Wax as it's environmentally friendly and can be washed out of the cloth at 60°C.

Our fifth book, Screen Printing, provides more detailed advice on how to use all of these resists. However, it's worth mentioning that Soy Wax can be applied by using techniques similar to those discussed in this book. You'll just need to dedicate some tools to the wax pot and if Soy Wax grabs you, invest in some specialist tools such as tjantings, which can be used for line work.

Georgeann scrapes thickened dye over soy wax resist

Soy wax resist followed by scraping with thickened Mx dyes (Cindy Kearney)

Resources/Suppliers

In terms of general supplies, dyes, paints, chemicals and tools, the web site (www.committedtocloth.com) has a list of suppliers, but the following companies will be able to provide you with what you need. If it's a web-based company, many ship worldwide but you may need to factor in import duty when comparing prices.

EUROPE

Ario
5 Pengry Road, Loughor, Swansea SA4 6PH
www.ario.co.uk

Art Van Go
The Studios, 1 Stevenage Road, Knebworth, Herts G3 6AN
www.artvango.co.uk

Atelier Tisch
In der Lache 18, 67308 Zellertal, Germany
www.ateliertisch.de

Atlantis Art
7-9 Plumber's Road, London E1 1EQ
www.atlantisart.co.uk

The Bramble Patch
West Street, Weedon, Northamptonshire NN7 4QU
www.thebramblepatch.co.uk

Fibrecrafts/George Weil
Old Portsmouth Road, Peasmarsh, Guildford, Surrey GU3 1LZ
www.fibrecrafts.co.uk

Jacksons Art Supplies
Arch 66, Station Approach, Fulham, London SW6 3U
1 Farleigh Place, London N16 7SX
www.jacksonsart.co.uk

Jeromin
A3, 5, 68159 Mannheim, Germany
www.jeromin-shop.de

Nannas Verksted
Skolebakken 29, 1628 Engelsviken, Norway
www.nannasverksted.no

Quiltstar (also provides a thermofax service)
Schnewlinstr. 5a, 79098 Freiberg, Germany
www.quiltstar.de

Quilt und Textile
Sebastiansplatz 4, Munich 80331, Germany
www.quiltundtextilkunst.de

Jayne-Willoughby-Scott: lines drawn with a needle-nose bottle, sprayed with liquid dyes

Patchwork Shop (also provides a thermofax service)
www.patchworkshop.de or www.pdpm.de

Spektrum Textil (also provides a thermofax service)
Radhusvej 2, 2920 Charlottenlund, Copenhagen, Denmark
www.spektrumtextil.dk

Stone Creek Silk (incorporating Thermofax-Online)
Stone Creek House, Sunk Island, East Yorkshire, HU12 0AP
www.stonecreeksilk.co.uk

Thermofax Screens (also supplies fabric paints)
Foxley Farm, Foxley, Towcester NN12 8HP
www.thermofaxscreens.co.uk

Thermofax Printing (also supplies fabric paints)
43 Southview Road, Southwick, East Sussex BN42 4TS
www.thermofaxprinting.co.uk

Whaleys
Harris Court, Great Horton, Bradford, West Yorkshire
www.whaleys-bradford.ltd.uk

Winifred Cottage
17 Elms Road, Fleet, Hampshire GU51 3EG
www.winifredcottage.co.uk

Zijdelings
Kapelstraat 93a, 5046 CL Tilberg, The Netherlands
www.zijdelings.com

NORTH AMERICA

Dick Blick (U.S.A.)
PO Box 1267, Galesburgh, IL 61402
www.dickblick.com

DIY Print Supply (thermofaxes and other print supplies, U.S.A.)
Welsh Products Inc, PO Box 6120, Arnold, CA 95223-6120
www.diyprintsupply.com

Dharma Trading Company (U.S.A.)
1604 Fourth Street, San Rafael, California 94901
www.dharmatrading.com

GS Dye (Canada)
250 Dundas Street West, No. 8, Toronto M5T 2Z5, Ontario
www.gsdye.com

Maiwa (Canada)
6-1666 Johnston Street, Granville Island, Vancouver V6H 3SZ, B.C.
www.maiwa.com

ProChemical & Dye (U.S.A.)
PO Box 14, Somerset, MA 02726
www.prochemical.com

Rupert, Gibbon & Spider (U.S.A.)
PO Box 452, Healdsburg, CA 95448
www.jacquardproducts.com

NEW ZEALAND & AUSTRALIA

Artbeat of Tasmania (Tasmania, Australia)
85 Channel Highway, Kingston, Tasmania 7050
www.artbeattas.com

Artisan Books (Australia)
159 Gertrude St, Fitzroy 3065, Victoria
www.artisan.com.au

Batik Oetoro (Australia)
8/9 Arnhem Close, Gateshead, NSW 2290
www.dyeman.com

Essential Textile Art (Australia)
PO Box 3416, Rundle Mall, SA 5000
www.essentialtextileart.com

KraftKolour (Australia)
Box 379, Whittlesea, Victoria 3757
www.kraftkolour.com.au

New Zealand Quilter (New Zealand)
PO Box 14567, Kilbirnie, Wellington 6241
www.nzquilter.co.nz

The Thread Studio (Australia)
6 Smith Street, Perth 6000
www.thethreadstudio.com

Further Reading

Surface Design
Many books are available on surface design and the use of different media, including the following:
Holly Brackman: The Surface Designers' Handbook, Interweave Press, 2008
Jane Dunnewold: Art Cloth; a guide to surface design for fabric, Interweave Press, 2010. Jane also has several self-published DVD's and 'books on CD' available from www.artclothstudios.com.
Rayna Gilman: Create your own hand-printed cloth, C&T Publishing, 2008
Ruth Issett: Colour on Paper & Fabric, Batsford 1998
Sherrill Kahn: Creating with Paint, Martingale & Company, 2001
Ann Johnston: Color by Accident (1997) and Color by Design (2001), self published
Jean Ray Laury: Imagery on Fabric, C&T Publishing, 1992.
Rheni Tauchid: The New Acrylics, Watson-Guptill, 2005
Kate Wells: Fabric Dyeing & Printing, Conran Octopus, 1997

Background imagery created with square foam blocks and pot lids. Hand quilted (Daline Stott)